Today's Sports Stars

# Jayden Daniels
## Football Star

Focus Readers
BEACON

by Luke Hanlon

# www.focusreaders.com

Copyright © 2026 by Focus Readers®, Mendota Heights, MN 55120. All rights reserved. No part of this book may be reproduced or utilized in any form or by any means without written permission from the publisher.

Focus Readers is distributed by North Star Editions:
sales@northstareditions.com | 888-417-0195

Produced for Focus Readers by Red Line Editorial.

Photographs ©: Stephanie Scarbrough/AP Images, cover, 1; Scott Taetsch/Getty Images Sport/Getty Images, 4, 22; Matt Patterson/AP Images, 6, 29; Shutterstock Images, 8; Louis Lopez/Cal Sport Media/ZUMA Press, Inc./AP Images, 11; David Rosenblum/Icon Sportswire/AP Images, 13; Christian Petersen/Getty Images Sport/Getty Images, 14; Jonathan Bachman/Getty Images Sport/Getty Images, 17; Michael Hickey/Getty Images Sport/Getty Images, 18; Mike Ehrmann/Getty Images Sport/Getty Images, 20; Michael Owens/Getty Images Sport/Getty Images, 25; Red Line Editorial, 27

### Library of Congress Cataloging-in-Publication Data

Names: Hanlon, Luke author
Title: Jayden Daniels : football star / by Luke Hanlon.
Description: Mendota Heights, MN: Focus Readers, 2026. | Series: Today's
    sports stars | Includes index. | Audience: Grades 2-3
Identifiers: LCCN 2025009662 (print) | LCCN 2025009663 (ebook) | ISBN
    9798889985914 hardcover | ISBN 9798889986171 paperback | ISBN
    9798889986089 pdf | ISBN 9798889986003 ebook
Subjects: LCSH: Daniels, Jayden, 2000---Juvenile literature | Quarterbacks
    (Football)--United States--Biography--Juvenile literature | LCGFT: Biographies
Classification: LCC GV939.D335 H36 2026  (print) | LCC GV939.D335  (ebook)
    | DDC 796.332092--dc23/eng/20250116
LC record available at https://lccn.loc.gov/2025009662
LC ebook record available at https://lccn.loc.gov/2025009663

Printed in the United States of America
Mankato, MN
082025

# About the Author

Luke Hanlon is a sportswriter and editor based in Minneapolis. He's written dozens of nonfiction sports books for kids and spends a lot of his free time watching his favorite Minnesota sports teams.

# Table of Contents

**CHAPTER 1**

## Playoff Push  5

**CHAPTER 2**

## Record Breaker  9

**CHAPTER 3**

## Ups and Downs  15

**CHAPTER 4**

## A Bright Future  21

At-a-Glance Map • 26

Focus Questions • 28

Glossary • 30

To Learn More • 31

Index • 32

# CHAPTER 1

# Playoff Push

Jayden Daniels sprinted toward the end zone. The Washington Commanders quarterback bounced off defenders. He made it all the way to the 2-yard line.

**The Washington Commanders played the Atlanta Falcons on December 29, 2024.**

**Daniels threw for three touchdowns against the Atlanta Falcons.**

The game was in **overtime**. Daniels needed a touchdown to beat the Atlanta Falcons. On the next play, the **rookie** scanned the field. He fired a pass to Zach Ertz. Fans roared as the tight end made a catch in the end zone.

The win clinched Washington's spot in the playoffs. Daniels had led the Commanders to their first postseason appearance in four years.

## Did You Know?

Jayden Daniels was used to dramatic finishes. In 2024, the Commanders won five games on the final play.

# CHAPTER 2
# Record Breaker

Jayden Daniels was born on December 18, 2000. He grew up in San Bernardino, California. Jayden loved football as a kid. He started playing when he was five years old.

**San Bernardino (pictured) is a suburb of Los Angeles, California.**

By high school, Jayden was a great athlete. As a **freshman**, he became Cajon High School's starting quarterback. He also ran track. That sport helped him get faster. On the football field, Jayden used his speed to escape defenders.

## Did You Know?

Jayden's dad had played cornerback in college. He wanted his son to play that position, too. But Jayden wanted to be on offense.

Jayden leaps over a defender during the 2017 state championship game.

Jayden could beat defenses with his arm, too. In 2017, he threw for 62 touchdowns. He also piled up 6,431 total yards of offense. That set a new California state record.

The young quarterback kept up his terrific play in the state tournament. In one playoff game, he threw for 293 yards. He also ran for 281 yards. Then, he lifted Cajon to a 70–23 blowout in the semifinals. However, Cajon lost in the championship game.

The next year, Jayden led Cajon back to the title game. Once again, the team fell short. But Jayden finished his high school career with a total of 17,406 offensive yards.

In January 2019, Jayden played in the Under Armour All-America Game.

Jayden had proven that he was one of the top **prospects** in the country. More than 20 colleges offered him a **scholarship**. Jayden decided to attend Arizona State University.

**CHAPTER 3**

# Ups and Downs

Jayden Daniels quickly showed that he was ready for college football. Right away, he became his team's starting quarterback. No first-year Arizona State player had done that before.

**Jayden Daniels lifted Arizona State to a 30–7 victory in his first college game.**

Daniels threw for 2,943 yards and 17 touchdowns in 2019. And he rarely made mistakes. He threw only two **interceptions** all year.

The next two seasons didn't go as well. Arizona State's offense didn't pass much. And the team struggled to **recruit** great players. Daniels wanted to show off his skills on a bigger stage. So, he transferred to Louisiana State University (LSU).

In 2022, Daniels helped the Tigers upset two teams ranked

**Daniels had two passing touchdowns and a rushing touchdown in an overtime win against No. 6 Alabama.**

in the top 10. Then, LSU played in the Citrus Bowl. Daniels led his team to a 63–7 win. After that, he decided to return to LSU for one more season.

Daniels threw 40 touchdown passes in 2023.

Daniels continued to improve in 2023. He rarely turned the ball over. And he led the nation with 4,946 total yards. After the season, Daniels won the Heisman Trophy.

That award goes to the best player in college football.

Daniels knew he was ready for the pros. The Washington Commanders agreed. The team selected the LSU star with the second pick in the 2024 National Football League (NFL) **Draft**.

## Did You Know?

Daniels spent his 23rd birthday helping kids in Louisiana. He donated 100 bikes and helmets.

# CHAPTER 4
# A Bright Future

In the NFL, Daniels found success right away. He quickly impressed his new coaches. They named him the starting quarterback. However, fans didn't expect much from the Commanders in 2024.

**Daniels ran for two touchdowns in his first NFL game.**

**Daniels recorded a season-high 326 passing yards in a Week 8 win against the Chicago Bears.**

Daniels surprised everyone. He led Washington to a hot start. In Week 3, he completed 91 percent of his passes. That set an NFL record for rookies. Washington won five of its first seven games.

Daniels got injured in Week 7. He played through the pain, though. Washington racked up two more wins. After that, the injury took its toll. The Commanders lost three games in a row. But Daniels soon bounced back. Washington ended the regular season strong. The team won its last five games.

The Commanders earned a spot in the playoffs. First, they faced the Tampa Bay Buccaneers. With four minutes left, the game was tied.

Daniels marched Washington's offense down the field. The Commanders scored a field goal as time ran out. It sealed the team's first playoff victory in 19 years.

Daniels didn't stop there. Washington faced the Detroit Lions next. Daniels threw two

## Did You Know?

Daniels won the Offensive Rookie of the Year Award in 2024. He was the first Washington player to win it since 2012.

Daniels set an NFL rookie record with 822 passing yards during the 2024 postseason.

touchdowns. He led his team to a huge upset. The Commanders finally got knocked out in the **conference** championship. But fans couldn't wait to see what Daniels would do next.

## AT-A-GLANCE MAP

# Jayden Daniels

- Height: 6 feet, 4 inches (193 cm)
- Weight: 210 pounds (95 kg)
- Birth date: December 18, 2000
- Birthplace: Fontana, California
- High school: Cajon High School (San Bernardino, California)
- College: Arizona State University (Tempe, Arizona) (2019–21); Louisiana State University (Baton Rouge, Louisiana) (2022–23)
- NFL team: Washington Commanders (2024–)
- Major awards: Heisman Trophy (2023); Pro Bowl (2024); NFL Offensive Rookie of the Year (2024)

# Focus Questions

*Write your answers on a separate piece of paper.*

1. Write a paragraph that explains the main ideas of Chapter 3.

2. What do you think is Jayden Daniels's biggest strength as a quarterback? Why?

3. Which team did the Commanders beat in Daniels's first NFL playoff game?
   - **A.** Atlanta Falcons
   - **B.** Tampa Bay Buccaneers
   - **C.** Philadelphia Eagles

4. What helped Jayden Daniels win the Heisman Trophy in 2023?
   - **A.** He led LSU to a championship.
   - **B.** He led the country in total yards.
   - **C.** He often turned the ball over.

**5.** What does **clinched** mean in this book?

*The win **clinched** Washington's spot in the playoffs. Daniels had led the Commanders to their first postseason appearance in four years.*

    **A.** made rare or unlikely
    **B.** blocked or removed
    **C.** assured or made certain

**6.** What does **dramatic** mean in this book?

*Jayden Daniels was used to **dramatic** finishes. In 2024, the Commanders won five games on the final play.*

    **A.** sad
    **B.** exciting
    **C.** boring

*Answer key on page 32.*

# Glossary

**conference**
A group of teams within a league.

**draft**
A system that allows teams to acquire new players coming into a league.

**freshman**
A first-year student.

**interceptions**
Plays in which the defense catches a pass, gaining possession of the ball.

**overtime**
An extra period to determine a winner in a tie game.

**prospects**
Players who are likely to be successful in the future.

**recruit**
To try to persuade someone to attend a college, usually to play sports.

**rookie**
A professional athlete in his or her first year.

**scholarship**
Money given to students to pay for education expenses.

# To Learn More

## BOOKS

Hanlon, Luke. *Washington Commanders*. Apex Editions, 2025.

Hewson, Anthony K. *Football Records*. Focus Readers, 2021.

Kelley, K. C. *LSU Tigers*. The Child's World, 2021.

## NOTE TO EDUCATORS

Visit **www.focusreaders.com** to find lesson plans, activities, links, and other resources related to this title.

# Index

**A**

Arizona State University, 13, 15–16

Atlanta Falcons, 6

**C**

Cajon High School, 10, 12

**D**

Detroit Lions, 24

draft, 19

**E**

Ertz, Zach, 7

**H**

Heisman Trophy, 18

**L**

Louisiana State University (LSU), 16–17, 19

**O**

overtime, 6

**P**

playoffs, 7, 12, 23–24

prospects, 13

**R**

rookies, 6, 22, 24

**S**

San Bernardino, California, 9

**T**

Tampa Bay Buccaneers, 23